THE HOI
AND FO

The Holy Shroud New Evidence Compared with the Visions of St. Bridget of Sweden, Maria d'Agreda, Catherine Emmerick, and Teresa Neumann.

By
Rev. Patrick O'Connell, B.D.
Columban Fathers, Dalgan Park,
Navan, Ireland.
And
Rev. Charles Carty
Radio Replies Press Society
St. Paul 1, Minn., U. S. A.

A Reply To The Parisian Surgeon Pierre Barbet, M. D.
Author of A DOCTOR AT CALVARY.

TAN BOOKS AND PUBLISHERS, INC.
Rockford, Illinois 61105

PREFACE

For the composition of this booklet the following books were consulted: *New Light on the Passion of Our Divine Lord* by Rev. Patrick O'Connell, B.D. Columban Fathers, Dalgan Park, Navan, Ireland. *Le Saint Suaire de Turin* by Dr. Paul Vignon (latest edition 1939), *Les Cinq Plaies* by Dr. Barbet, *Le Christ Dans Sa Passion Revele Par Le Saint Suaire de Turin* by Gerard Cordonnier, *Golgotha* by Dr. Hynek; three articles by Fr. Wuenschel, C. SS. R. in *American Ecclesiastical Review 1953; The Holy Shroud* by Dr. Beecher; four articles in *Revue Metaphysique 1938; La Santa Sindone Rivelata Dalla Fotografia* by Cav. G. Enrie; *The Burial of Christ* by Professor Alfred O'Rahilly; *The Holy Shroud of Jesus Christ* by Lieut-Colonel P. W. Gorman; *The Holy Shroud of Turin* by Stella Bellars; *La S. Sindone* by Dr. Luigi Lovera Di Maria; *A Doctor at Calvary* by Dr. Pierre Barbet, Fr. Wuenschel's latest book, *Self-Portrait of Christ* and the principal books of St. Bridget of Sweden, Venerable Maria d'Agreda, Anne Catherine Emmerich and Teresa Neumann have also been consulted.

The object of this pamphlet is to throw light on the visions of the Passion from the evidence of the Holy Shroud and to show that the sufferings of Our Divine Lord in His Passion were far greater than they are generally represented in sermons and books.

We hold that the image on the Holy Shroud which records in minute detail the terrible story of the Passion is not the result of accident but the work of Providence.

Two events occurred towards the close of the last century which rescued the Shroud from the tomb of oblivion in which it was lying in its shrine at Turin and led to a thorough investigation of its history, of the image upon it, of how it was formed and of what the image reveals. These two events were first; the discovery by Canon Ulisses Chevalier of evidence that a copy of the Shroud had been painted back about 1350, which started a controversy as to whether this painted copy and the Shroud of Turin were identical, and second; the taking of the first photograph of the Shroud by Secundo Pia in 1898.

When the Shroud was exposed for veneration in 1931 and 1933, doctors and other scientists endorsed the verdict of the French scientists that the Holy Shroud of Turin was *Not a Painting,* but truly the Shroud in which Joseph and Nicodemus wrapped the Body of Our Lord.

The following statement of Pope Pius XI was published in the *Osservatore Romano* on Sept. 7, 1936: "The Holy Shroud of Turin is still mysterious, but it is certainly not the work of any human hand. This, one can now say, is demonstrated. We said mysterious, because the sacred object still involves many problems, but certainly it is more sacred than perhaps any other; and, as is now established in the most positive way, even apart from any idea of faith or Christian piety, it is certainly not a human work." In all, thirty-three Popes have spoken in favor of the Shroud, among whom are Leo XIII, Pius X, Pius XI, and Pius XII.

History of the Holy Shroud

The following is the combined account of the Four Evangelists and the Holy Shroud; Joseph of Arimathea bought a length of linen sufficient to make the shroud mentioned by the Synoptics and to furnish the linen cloths mentioned by St. John. He then cut off about fourteen feet and a half for the Shroud that was to cover the Body from head to foot, front and back, and divided the remainder into two or three lengths to go around the Body outside the Shroud. He next stretched the fourteen and a half feet length on the ground, sprinkled the myrrh and aloes over it and laid the Body of Our Lord upon it with the Head towards the middle and the feet about a foot and a half from one end. He turned this foot and a half over Our Lord's feet and legs half way up to the knees. (We know that this was done because there is no image of the front of the feet on the Shroud. This foot and a half has disappeared having probably been given away by the Emperor of Constantinople as a relic). He then drew the other end over the head and covered the front of the Body including the feet. (On this front portion there is only the mark of blood which flowed from the feet). Both from St. John and from the Shroud itself we infer that the Shroud was not left loose: St. John says that they bound the Body of Jesus in linen cloths, and the image on the Shroud shows that it was in close contact with the Body except in a few places—the neck and the front of the shoulders. These bands or pieces of linen have disappeared.

In his account of the burial, St. John does not refer expressly to the Shroud, but in his account of the linens found in the tomb after the Resurrection he refers to two kinds. He says that the Beloved Disciple and St. Peter saw the linen cloths (which had been around the Body) lying (this, we may presume, means that they had not been untied); but the *Sudarium*

4

that had been about His head (or drawn over the head) not lying with the other cloths but apart, wrapped up in one place. It is highly probable that this piece of linen which St. John singles out for mention, and which Our Lord Himself detached from the other linens, folded up and laid apart, was the Holy Shroud.

St. John says that the burial of Our Lord was carried out according to the manner of the Jews, but this does not mean that the Jewish manner of burial was absolutely uniform, or that everything done at a Jewish burial was carried out. The Shroud shows that the Jewish custom of passing a cloth under the chin and tying it on top of the head was carried out, for there is a gap in the image of the head on the Shroud where it passed over the knot; the Jewish custom of stretching out the fingers and turning the thumbs into the palm of the hand was also observed. The use of the shroud itself and the way it was tied was also a Jewish custom except among the poor who were buried in their clothes. The Body of Our Lord was not anointed, Mary Magdalen had anointed it for His burial, nor was the Body washed.

Brief History of the Holy Shroud

No reference to the Holy Shroud has so far been found in early Christian literature during the first three centuries of persecution. There were many reasons for the silence. Any reference to it might lead to its discovery by the enemies of Christianity. Besides, during these three centuries of persecution while the cross was still used as an instrument for the execution of slaves and criminals, it was forbidden by the Ecclesiastical authorities to paint or display an image of Christ on the cross. This prohibition would virtually extend to the exhibition of the Holy Shroud which gives a vivid representation of the whole Passion with its most terrible and humiliating details. It was not until 692 A.D. that the Council of Constantinople decreed that the image of Christ Himself represented alive on the cross should replace the image of the Lamb. It was not until the tenth century that permission was given to represent Him dead on the cross.

We have conclusive evidence that the Holy Shroud of Turin is the same as that exhibited at Constantinople for hundreds of years; and as the scientific evidence in favor of the Shroud is now accepted as sufficient to prove that it was the Shroud in which the Body of Our Lord was wrapped, we can say the same of the Shroud of Constantinople. The Byzantine historian of the fourteenth century, Nicephorus Callista, gives the following account of how the Holy Shroud came to Constantinople: "Pulcheria the Empress of the East (399-453) having built a Basilica at Blachernes (outside Constantinople), in 436 A.D., piously deposited there the burial linens of the Blessed Virgin and the linens of Our Saviour which had just been re-discovered, and which the Empress Eudoxia had sent to her."

Mgr. Barnes in his book on the Shroud contributes an interesting proof that the Shroud of Turin and the Shroud of Constantinople are identical and that both are genuine. It is the following:

There was a tradition in the East before the time of the Crusades that Christ was lame, which tradition is embodied in the Byzantine Cross. Due to the fact that the left foot of Our Lord was nailed over the right, thus causing the left leg to be bent, and the fact that the *Rigor Mortis* (as appears evident from the Shroud) had set in before Our Lord was taken down from the cross, and left the leg bent up, the leg on the Shroud appears to be two inches shorter than the right. Those missionaries who saw the Shroud in Constantinople and went to preach the Gospel in the East, not having the aid of

6

photography, failed to see the reason why one leg appears to be shorter than the other on the image on the Shroud and incidentally provide us with evidence that the Shroud that was kept at Blachernes outside Constantinople for hundreds of years is the same Shroud which is now in Turin.

The Byzantine Cross consists of one upright and three cross-bars. The upper cross-bar represents the board on which the title was written, the middle one, which is the longest, the cross-beam to which Our Lord's hands were nailed and the lower one, which is slanting, the board which was thought to have been placed under Our Lord's feet. This is placed slanting at an angle, because those who designed the Byzantine Cross, through a mistaken interpretation of the imprint of Our Lord's feet on the Holy Shroud, imagined that the left leg was shorter than the right. Though there was probably a small piece of wood between Our Lord's feet and the cross, it was not as a support for the feet but to fill up the vacant space under the heel. This is proved by the fact that the feet are stretched down so that Our Lord's Body appears to be six inches longer than it really is.

There is historic evidence that the Emperors of Constantinople showed the Shroud to many distinguished visitors between 1171 and 1203 A.D. Among these were Bishop William of Tyre and King Amaury of Jerusalem. It was exposed for veneration every Friday at the time of the Crusades. The fact that there had been a prohibition to depict Christ dead upon the cross would explain why it had not been exposed for veneration at an earlier date, but this would not prevent priests and other important people from seeing it privately.

How the Holy Shroud Came to France

At the time of the fourth Crusade, Otho de la Roche, Duke of Athens and Sparta, who was in command of the district of

Blachernes where the Shroud was kept, received it as part of his recompense. He sent it to his father in 1204 A.D. and his father gave it to the Bishop of Besancon who placed it in the Cathedral. It was exposed for veneration each year on Easter Sunday up till 1349. In that year a fire broke out in the Cathedral which caused slight damage to the Holy Shroud. To save it from further damage it was removed from the Cathedral and in the confusion it was stolen and given to King Philip of France. King Philip gave it to his friend Geoffrey Count of Charney and Lord of Liry. It was natural that the Bishop of Besancon should try to recover the Shroud, but as the King of France had given it to his friend, it was impossible for him to do so. Two years later a painted copy began to be exhibited in the Cathedral of Besancon to satisfy the devotion of those who had been accustomed to venerate the real Shroud; about the same time, probably a little earlier, Geoffrey of Liry employed a painter to paint a copy. Dom Chamard found conclusive evidence that the Shroud exhibited at Besancon after 1352 was only a painting—but a painting which had been copied from the real Shroud. He adds, "Dunod in his *History of the Church of Besancon* speaks of the Shroud preserved in the Cathedral of St. Etienne (Besancon) in the thirteenth century, and proceeds thus: 'In March, 1349, the church was destroyed by fire, and the box in which the Holy Shroud was kept, seemingly without much formality, was lost. Some years afterwards the relic was found again by happy chance, and to make sure that it was the same as was formerly venerated in the church of St. Etienne, it was laid upon a dead man, who immediately revived. The fact of this miracle is established not only by the records of the church of Besancon but also by a manuscript preserved up to the present time in the church of St. James, at Rheims, where it has been placed by Richard La Pie, senior priest of Besancon, in the year 1375, who had been himself an eye-witness.' "

Mgr. Barnes relates that in the church of St. Gomaire, in Belgium, there is a copy of the Shroud which was made in 1516 and consequently had not the marks of the fire of 1532 at Chambery. In this copy there are to be seen traces of an earlier fire in 1349 at Besancon. This evidence identifies the Shroud with the one that was in Besancon as early as 1208.

How the Shroud Came into the Possession of the House of Savoy

During the hundred years war Margaret, the grand-daughter of Geoffrey, took the Shroud from the Canons of Liry for safe keeping to her husband's castle. When later on in 1452, the Canons wanted to get it back, she refused to give it to them but instead sent it to her cousin, Anna, the daughter of the King of Cyprus, who was then living at Chambery with her husband, Duke Louis I of Savoy. Two years later, Pope Sixtus IV authorized Louis I to build a sanctuary at his residence at Chambery to house the Shroud. His Successor, Julius II, in the Bull *Romanus Pontifex,* issued in 1506, formally approved an Office and Mass of the Holy Shroud of Turin.

At the beginning of the following century, on Good Friday 1503, the Shroud was brought to the neighboring town of Bourg-en-Bresse for the convenience of Archduke Philip of Austria who passed that way. On that occasion, in order to show that the image on the Shroud was truly the image of Christ, the Shroud was submitted to an ordeal: it was first plunged into boiling oil, then it was put in water and boiled over a fire and finally washed several times. It was believed that if the Shroud was genuine the image of Our Lord would not be effaced.

Troubled times followed and the Shroud was moved from one place to another in France. It was brought back to

Chambery again and there, on the night of December 3rd 1532, it nearly perished in another fire. Four men: two Franciscan Fathers, the Duke's butler and a blacksmith broke the locks, the other three poured water on the Shroud. In spite of their efforts the Shroud, which was folded upon itself twelve times, got burned at the two ends of the folds by hot molten silver. When it was opened out to full length it showed sixteen holes of considerable size and twelve smaller ones. Fortunately not much damage was done to the image of Our Lord. The holes were repaired by the Poor Clare Nuns of Chambery.

As we have already seen, without the aid of Divine Providence we would not have this image of Christ in His sufferings, and we can say with equal truth without the protection of Divine Providence it could not have survived during the early persecutions, subsequent wars and revolutions and dangers from fire and water. The ordeal to which it was submitted in 1503, which has recently been brought to light, not only proves that it is not the painting that was made in 1351, but that Providence used this very ordeal to make the image clearer and more distinct.

In 1578 the Shroud was brought to Turin in order to save the aged St. Charles Borromeo the trouble of journeying to Chambery to venerate it. It has remained in Turin since then, having been kept in the chapel of the castle until 1694 when it was transferred to the black marble chapel built specially for it behind the Cathedral, where it is still kept.

It was venerated by St. Francis de Sales in 1613 and by St. Jane Frances de Chantal in 1639. Up to the year 1800, it was exposed for veneration each year on the feast of the Finding of the Holy Cross. From 1800 to 1900, it was exposed only six times, the last of which was in 1898 when it was photographed for the first time. Since then it has been exposed only twice: in 1931 and 1933, on each of which occasions the fullest opportunity was given to experts to examine it carefully and photograph it.

The Two Images on the Holy Shroud

When the Holy Shroud was photographed for the first time in 1898, it was discovered with amazement that the plate when developed contained a true positive image much clearer than that on the Shroud, and, in addition, the usual negative indications in white of the dark stains made by the Precious Blood on the Shroud. Those who saw it were astonished above all at the marvellous image of the Holy Face revealing a majesty and beauty such as no artist has ever been able to depict. The image, then, which can be seen on the Shroud itself, and which appears blurred and indistinct, is really a perfect negative and contains in addition a positive image of all the wounds of Our Lord. We can therefore say that there are two double images; one on the Shroud, the other on the negative. A negative image invisible to the eye and a positive image made by the Precious Blood are found on the Shroud itself, and a positive image of Our Lord and a negative image of the traces of the Precious Blood on the developed negative.

How the Images Were Formed

It was taken for granted up to 1898, when the Shroud was photographed, that the image on it was formed in the ordinary way by contact of the Shroud with the Body of Our Divine Lord covered with wounds and blood. It was not, however, till a number of scientists began to make experiments to find out how the wonderful image that appeared on the negative was formed, that it was discovered that were it not for the myrrh and aloes and the sweat of the Passion that remained on the Body, the Blood which had dried on the sacred

Body would not have been transferred to the Shroud, and that we would have had no image on it, only the marks of the Blood that flowed from the hands and feet when the nails were removed, and from the deep wound on the side that was reopened by the moving of the Body.

The scientists have learned from their experiments that the image on the Shroud could not have been produced by painting, that it contained so many unexpected details—the place of the nails in the hands and feet, the thumbs turned in on the palms of the hands, the wound of the lance on the right side, the feet turned in, the left leg seemingly shorter than the right, the distinctive marks on the Holy Face, the unsuspected hidden image—that no forger could have possibly thought of half of them. They discovered that nothing less than the complete set of circumstances surrounding the burial and resurrection of Our Lord would be sufficient to account for the image. In the first place there would be required the dead body covered with sweat of a person who had been scourged from head to foot, crowned with thorns, crucified, pierced with a lance on the right side and left on the cross after death until the *Rigor Mortis* had set in. There would be required in addition a linen shroud of unusual thickness, not lying loose but carefully bound around so as to be in close contact with the body, and sprinkled over with a rich mixture of myrrh and aloes. Finally there would be required that the body remain in the tomb not much less and not much more than a day and a half, and that some one should come just at the right time and detach the Shroud with more than human skill and caution so as not to blur the image.

The scientists carried out experiments to discover in what circumstances blood that had dried on an object would be transferred from the object to a linen cloth and at the same time leave an image of the object on the cloth. They found that the dried blood would not be transferred at all without the aid of some chemical substance; that myrrh and aloes alone were not sufficient but that something must be added to represent the chemical components of sweat. They found that to form a clear image, just as to print a photograph, a definite length of time was required; if the time was too short, there was either no image at all or a faint image, if the time was too long the image would become blurred and ultimately destroyed. They found that the cloth must be detached very carefully so as not to blur the image and that it must not be folded too soon, for if so the blood would peel off in scales. The experts are agreed on the point that in addition to myrrh and aloes something such as ammonia or turpentine to represent the chemical components of human sweat is necessary. Some scientists believe that the image is transferred by vaporization, but Professor Judica Cordiglio thinks it was by oxidization. It is very probable that a cloth was wound round the Sacred Head *outside* the shroud, for otherwise the image would not have been so clear.

The Shroud Compared with the Writings of St. Bridget of Sweden and Other Contemplatives

Of the visions of the Passion that have come down to us the most complete are those of St. Bridget of Sweden, Venerable Maria d'Agreda, Anne Catherine Emmerich and Teresa Neumann. The evidence of the Holy Shroud and the details of the visions of these four women on the physical sufferings of Our Lord is the object of this pamphlet.

Accounts of the visions of these four have been published with *Imprimatur* in many languages, and have been widely read. The visions of the Passion by St. Bridget of Sweden and Venerable Maria d'Agreda have been used by Fr. Gallwey,

S.J., in the composition of the *Watches of the Passion*.
Visions of the Passion are rarely quoted by commentators on
Sacred Scripture and, if quoted, are generally dismissed as
mere pious contemplations of holy souls who see the events
of the Passion according to their own preconceived ideas. The
discrepancies that have been found in the visions of the Passion by different people, and which are principally due to
errors in recording, have been very much magnified. There
are only a few discrepancies in the four accounts we are about
to consider and these discrepancies are easily explained.

St. Bridget of Sweden

St. Bridget of Sweden belonged to a noble Swedish family.
She lived from 1303 to 1373. In her youth she was given in
marriage to a pious nobleman. The first two years of their
married life were spent in prayer and penance under a vow of
continence. Eight children were subsequently born of the
marriage and when they had grown up, both husband and
wife entered monasteries. After her husband's death, St.
Bridget founded the famous double monastery of Vadstena
on the shores of Loch Vetter. Later on, in the year 1349,
urged by a divine command, she went to Rome where she remained for the rest of her life and exercised a powerful influ-
ence on the events of her time. She led a most austere life
from her youth, and was favored with visions and revelations
during the greater part of her life. These were committed to
writing, partly by herself and partly by her confessors, and
were all translated into Latin by her confessor, Fr. Peter
Olafsson, who, at her invitation, went to Rome in 1350. They
were divided into eight books and cover the whole life of Our
Lord and of Our Blessed Lady. Those dealing with the Passion
are found in Books I, IV and VII. On just two questions are
there apparent contradictions in the accounts of St. Bridget

herself. The two questions are: whether three or four nails were used, and whether Our Lord was crucified on the ground or after the cross was erected. Her own account, which is repeated three times, is that the feet of Our Lord were crossed before they were nailed, which mode of crucifixion demands only three nails. After her account, it is added that four nails were used. This addition was probably made by her confessor, because it was the more common opinion that four nails were used—one for each wound. The account of the crucifixion given in Book VII, representing Christ as being crucified after the cross was erected, appears to be an addition of a later date.

The Venerable Maria d'Agreda

The Venerable Maria d'Agreda was born in Spain in 1602 and died in 1665. She belonged to a very remarkable family; her father and two brothers entered the Franciscan Order and the paternal home was turned into a convent which the mother and her two daughters, Maria and her sister, entered. Maria lived a very holy life; she took but one meal a day, slept only two hours at night, and practised most rigorous austerities. She was favored with visions and revelations about the Passion of Our Lord, the other events of His life and the life of Our Blessed Lady. Most of these revelations are found in a book called *The Mystical City.*

Anne Catherine Emmerich

Anne Catherine Emmerich was born in Westphalia in 1774, and died in 1824. The family to which she belonged was of the small farming class. Like Teresa Neumann she spent part of her youth as a servant maid. In the church of her native parish of Coesfeld there is a famous crucifix, much the same in shape as the cross on the Gothic chasuble. The arms of the figure on this crucifix do not fit to the arms of the cross, but

15

are extended, while the arms of Our Lord on the cross as seen by her later on, by St. Bridget of Sweden and by Teresa Neumann fit exactly to the arms of the cross which slope upwards. It cannot therefore be said that the vision of Our Lord on a cross, the arms of which sloped upwards, was nothing more than the Coesfeld cross seen in her imagination.

In 1802 she entered the convent of the Augustinians at Dulmen, and 1811 she was forced to leave along with the other Sisters when King Jerome Bonaparte suppressed all the convents in his kingdom. In 1812 she received the stigmata on her hands, feet, side and head. A cross of the shape that she saw in her visions was imprinted on her breast. From that date till her death, ten years later, she took no solid food. She had visions of the Passion accompanied with corresponding sufferings, and visions of other events in the life of Our Lord and of Our Blessed Lady.

A pious layman named Clement Brentano, who was also a poet, spent four years noting down her visions. As he gives the visions in his own poetical language, it is inevitable that there should be inaccuracies, but these have been greatly exaggerated. The account of the Passion given in Brentano's rendering of her visions corresponds in all important details with the evidence from the Holy Shroud. An excellent English translation of Brentano's work under the title of *The Dolorous Passion of Our Lord Jesus Christ* by Anne Catherine Emmerich has been published by Messrs. Burns Oates & Washbourne.

Teresa Neumann

Teresa Neumann was born on Good Friday 1898. The daughter of a small landholder and tailor, and the eldest of ten children, she was called upon to assist her parents even during her school-days to earn sufficient to support her little brothers and sisters. For the first nineteen years of her life she was remarkable for robust health, great physical strength, bright humor and deep piety. It was arranged by her and agreed to by her parents that she should enter a missionary order of Sisters for Central Africa as soon as the first world war was over. She prepared herself for religious life by following a rule of life based on the little way of St. Teresa of Lisieux for whose beatification she prayed. However, in 1918, she strained her spine by overexertion, and as a result of the injury she fell several times on her head and became blind. Paralysis ensued and, being completely bed-ridden and helpless, she became covered with sores. Besides, her digestive system was completely ruined and she contracted bronchitis and finally pneumonia.

Her blindness was cured on the day of the Beatification of the Little Flower; a leg that was to be amputated was healed by the application of leaves from the grave of the Little Flower; her paralysis and the other ulcers on the day of the Canonization; her appendicitis by applying a relic of the Little Flower; and, finally, her pneumonia on the anniversary of the death of the Little Flower. She had been paralyzed for six and a half years; when she was cured, a voice which she believed to be that of St. Teresa of Lisieux told her that she was cured but would have still greater suffering. In 1926, she received the stigmata first in the form of the Five Wounds, and later she received in addition the marks of the Crown of Thorns, the wound on the shoulder, the marks of the scourging and wounds on her knees corresponding to those of Our Lord caused by falling under the cross. From 1926 she has lived without earthly food on the Blessed Sacrament alone. The stigmata and the complete fast from food and drink have continued without a break until the present day.

Once a week, except during Paschaltide and Christmastide,

beginning at 11:00 p.m. on Thursday night and lasting until about 1:00 p.m. on Friday, she has a vision of the Passion of Our Lord in about forty scenes with short intervals, and experiences suffering corresponding to the various scenes—The Agony, the dungeon of Caiphas, the Scourging, Crowning with Thorns, Carrying of the Cross and Crucifixion. During Lent, all the stigmata bleed profusely; outside Lent, except on the Feast of the Sacred Heart, only the stigmata of the crown of thorns, of the wound in the side, and the eyes bleed.

Her stigmata are the most complete of any stigmatist of whom we have record. The stigmata on her hands and feet resemble those of St. Francis of Assisi in that they are in the form of fleshy nails that pierce the hands and feet, with the appearance of the square stem of the nail at one side of the point clinched at the other.

In 1927, her Bishop, Dr. Henle, had a complete investigation of all the phenomena of her case carried out by four Franciscan Sisters and two doctors. The result was declared by him to be completely satisfactory.

In 1928, His Holiness Pope Pius XI, who took a personal interest in her case, sent Dr. Gemelli, Rector of Milan University, to make an independent investigation. In his report he stated that there was no trace of hysteria, as some adversaries had alleged, and that no natural explanation of the phenomena was possible. Soon after receiving Dr. Gemelli's report, His Holiness sent her His Apostolic Blessing through the Apostolic Nuncio in Munich, Archbishop Pacelli, now Pope Pius XII, and in 1938 he sent her a relic of St. Francis of Assisi. During Holy Week of 1955, Pius XII sent her a relic of the True Cross.

Visits to her were prohibited by the Bavarian Bishops during the Nazi regime from 1937 until the end of the war. When the war ended, the restrictions that had been placed on visits were removed. Her Bishop has declared that permission from him to visit her is no longer necessary.

Like most of God's servants, Teresa Neumann has been the object of attack and hostile criticism by a small minority. Of about a hundred books and articles written about the phenomena in her life, eighty hold that these phenomena are works of Divine Providence; the remaining twenty, of which ten are by atheists, endeavor to find a natural explanation. The authors of books against Teresa Neumann in the German language are now all dead and so the controversy in Germany may be said to be over.

Books about Teresa Neumann that have been published in most countries outside Germany up to the last world war give the views of the eighty per cent majority—that the phenomena in her life demand a supernatural explanation.

In the case of Teresa Neumann, five Cardinals including the Cardinal Patriarch of Bavaria, thirty archbishops and bishops and a number of priests and eminent doctors, all of whom have made careful personal investigation of the phenomena, have published their views stating that these phenomena demand a supernatural explanation in her case.

Their views can be safely accepted by the laity, subject of course to any decision that the Holy See may ultimately make.

Teresa Neumann's visions of the Passion of Our Saviour are in agreement with those of St. Bridget of Sweden, Venerable Maria d'Agreda and Anne Catherine Emmerich, and with the evidence from the Holy Shroud of Turin.

The account of Teresa's visions which we are following was dictated by her to Fr. Leopold Witt, Parish Priest of a neighboring parish in the presence of Fr. Naber. It is, however, only a summary, but it is very valuable as it was written down in 1926 soon after her visions began, and is therefore free from the suspicion of having been influenced by the questions of visitors.

As already mentioned, her visions, which generally last for about fourteen hours, are not continuous, but are divided into about forty scenes with corresponding interruptions. Particular scenes sometimes last longer than usual; on these occasions, she gives details not mentioned in her previous accounts; otherwise, her visions of the Passion at present are exactly the same as they were thirty years ago.

The Holy Face

The Four Evangelists and the Prophet Isaias give us a lengthy and detailed account of the sufferings inflicted on the Holy Face; the Shroud of Turin not only confirms their account but reveals the majesty of that Face, from which the Divinity was not separated even in death, in a way that no human artist will ever equal.

What the Evangelists Tell Us

"Then did they spit on His Face and buffeted Him, and others struck Him in the Face with the palms of their hands, saying: Prophesy, O Christ, who is he that struck thee." (Matt. XXVI, 67, 68.)

"And some began to spit on Him and to cover His Face and to buffet Him, and to say to Him: Prophesy." (Mark, XIV, 65.)

"And the men that held Him mocked Him and struck Him. And they blindfolded Him and smote Him on the Face. And they asked Him, saying: Prophesy who it is that struck thee? And blaspheming, many other things they said against Him." (Luke, XXII, 63.)

One of the servants standing by gave Jesus a blow, saying: "Answerest thou the high priest so?" (John, XVIII, 22.)

The Prophet Isaias

"From the sole of the foot unto the top of the head, there is no soundness therein: wounds and bruises and swelling sores. They are not bound up, nor dressed nor fomented with oil." (Isaias I, 6.)

"I have given my body to the strikers and my cheeks to them that plucked them: I have not turned away my face from them that rebuked me and spit upon me." (Isaias L, 6.)

"Despised and the most abject of men, a man of sorrows and acquainted with infirmity; and his look was, as it were, hidden and despised, wherefore we esteemed him not.

"Surely he hath borne our infirmities and carried our sorrows, and we have thought him as it were a leper, and one struck by God and afflicted."

"But he was wounded for our iniquities and bruised for our sins." (Isaias, LIII, 3,4,5.)

If we look at the positive image on the Holy Shroud, we see at once that it affords full confirmation of the words of the Four Evangelists and of the prophecy of Isaias. The Holy Face is covered with blood and wounds, the nose is bruised, the cheeks are swollen, the beard and hair, in disorder. In the dungeon of Caiphas where Our Lord was bound tightly, the ministers of Satan struck Him on the Face with all their might; during the scourging, as we shall see later on, the Body of Our Lord was turned and His Face, which was exposed to the instruments of torture used to scourge Him, did not escape.

The image on the Shroud is an image that was transferred when the Face was cold in death and when the swellings had subsided at least partially. What appearance then must have that Face presented to Our Blessed Lady as she gazed upon it from beneath the Cross and watched the precious Blood trickling down from the wounds made by the Crown of Thorns!

The image on the photographic negative, which is really a positive, reveals the majestic appearance of the Holy Face in death. A Spanish member of the Commission of the Holy Shroud writes as follows about that negative image: "All scientists who have studied the mystery of the Holy Shroud have been amazed at the extraordinary appearance of the countenance of the dead Figure over which even in its terrible sufferings there reigns a heroic and resigned patience, a serenity of aspect, a will to sacrifice and suffer and complete resignation. There is no trace of anger or protest against the suffering inflicted. From that Holy Face, there radiates a sublime majesty as if something supernatural existed beyond it—something that sorrow and death have been able to reach without, however, being able to efface its immortal presence. . . . . ."

It may be said that if we had only the accounts of the Evangelists and of the Prophet Isaias we could scarcely have imagined that the Holy Face would have presented such a mutilated appearance as the Holy Shroud reveals. The visions of the Contemplatives, however, tell the same story of the wounds inflicted on the Holy Face as the Shroud. They tell us that, in addition to the blows inflicted on Our Lord's Face in the dungeon of Caiphas, during the scourging the Body of Our Divine Lord was turned round facing the executioners and His Face was scourged with rods or sticks; furthermore, they tell us that Our Lord fell more than three times under the Cross on the sorrowful way and that His Face was bruised and wounded by the rough stones on which He fell.

The General Impression of the Scourging Conveyed by the Holy Shroud

The image of Our Divine Lord's Body imprinted on the Holy Shroud recalls at once the prophecy of Isaias: "From the sole of the foot unto the top of the head, there is no soundness therein; wounds and bruises and swelling sores." (Isaias, I, 6.)

Dr. R. W. Hynek, (*Golgotha,* Karlsruhe, 1952) records his impressions of the image of Our Lord on the Holy Shroud as follows: "No pious phantasy, no lively imagination could invent what meets our eyes as stark reality. The innumerable wounds and marks with which the whole Body is covered convey an overpowering impression of the extreme suffering inflicted. Here for the first time is found an actual representation of the effects of the cruel scourging of ancient times.... The dead Body of the Man that was wrapped in this Shroud had been scourged and tortured before His death in a manner that has never before been even imagined, and the bloody traces upon it reveal to us the terrible nature of the awful death by crucifixion. The whole Body, both front and back, is covered with wounds so numerous that they cannot be counted: there are wounds on the breast, the abdomen, the thighs and the legs; on both shoulders, the loins, the hips and the calves of the legs. The wounds cross and re-cross each other over the whole Body, so that no sound spot remains. (*Golgotha,* pp. 125, 126.)

Further Details That the Holy Shroud Reveals

There is evidence from the Holy Shroud (1) that Our Lord *was standing up straight,* not bent down during the scourging; (2) that *His Body was turned* and that he was scourged on both the front and the back; (3) that the *executioners were in pairs;* and (4) *that more than one kind of instrument was used* in the scourging and probably *more than one pair of executioners.*

The evidence from the Holy Shroud *that Our Lord was standing up* during the scourging is (1) that there are no marks of the scourges on the fore-arm such as we find on the legs and (2) that the marks of the scourges on the shoulders slope upwards, those on the middle of the Body are horizontal and those on the legs slope downwards. The evidence that the Body was turned is that the marks on the front of the Body both left and right correspond to those on the back, and could hardly have been made from behind. The marks on both front and back indicate *that there was a pair of executioners.* The marks of the scourging on the back of the Shroud appear clearer and better defined because the weight of the Body pressed down on the under part of the Shroud beneath. The absence of marks from the side of the Body shows that it was not bound tightly by the strips of cloth outside, but is hardly sufficient to prove that there were no strips of cloth (as St. John says), because while the Shroud lay on the chest and front of the Body, it would naturally recede from the sides unless tied tightly. From the great number of wounds that appear all over the Body we would infer that there was more than one pair of executioners. As we shall see, the contemplatives agree in saying that they saw three pairs of executioners in their visions.

There is very clear evidence on the Shroud that more than one kind of scourge was used. There is no difficulty in identifying the marks of the typical Roman scourge called the *Flagrum.* The *Flagrum* consisted of a wooden handle to which were attached two or three leathern thongs tipped with balls of metal. These metal balls made a deep wound but according to some commentators (e.g., Dr. Primrose) the number of strokes with this instrument of torture was limited because otherwise the victim would die of its effect. However, there are marks of this terrible instrument of torture over Our Lord's whole Body front and back from the shoulders to the feet. Besides these deep round marks which are in pairs, there are long marks at regular intervals like ridges and furrows. The long wounds or furrows that the Holy Shroud shows were not made by the thongs of the *Flagrum* but by heavy rods or some other instruments of torture. This is corroborated by the visions of the contemplatives. It is customary still in the East to beat prisoners with heavy bamboo poles. These are dreaded far more than rods or whips, for they affect the whole frame, and cause the temperature to rise. According to the visions of the contemplatives these also were used in scourging Our Lord.

The Description of the Scourging by the Contemplatives

Let us now see how the four persons whose visions we are considering describe the scourging.

St. Bridget does not tell us whether she had a direct vision of the scourging, but records Our Lady's revelation to her concerning it as follows:

"Then led to the pillar, My Son stripped Himself, and He Himself stretched His hands to the pillar, which His enemies pitilessly bound. They scourged His body pure from all spot or stain . . . His whole body was lacerated with scourges tipped with sharp points turned back, not pulling out, but ploughing up . . . At the first blow, I, who stood nearest, fell as if dead, and on recovering my senses, I beheld His body bruised and beaten to the very ribs so that the ribs could be seen. And, what was still more bitter, when the scourge was raised, His very flesh was furrowed with the thongs. My Son stood thus, all bloody, all torn, so that no soundness could be found on Him nor any spot to scourge." (Books I and IV.)

The account by Teresa Neumann is much more detailed than the above account even as given in Fr. Leopold Witt's book. She says that His hands were bound to the top of a high pillar and that His Body was stretched; and He was scourged by two men at the same time, and that these were changed twice so that there were six executioners; that the Body was turned and was scourged in front also. In a later account she added that each pair of executioners made use of different instruments of torture, but her description of these instruments has not yet been published.

The following account given by her in 1926 to Fr. Leopold Witt and published by him in 1928 corresponds closely with the evidence from the Holy Shroud:

"After a while, I see Jesus being stripped for the scourging, and the terrible scourging itself. The pillar to which Our Saviour is bound is rather tall. He is suspended by His hands but only so that the body is stretched tight. Our Saviour stands on the ground. He is mercilessly scourged by two men at the same time. Those who scourge Him resemble those who took Him prisoner in the Garden of Olives. The executioners are changed twice so that actually six men scourge Him. Our dear Saviour is scourged all over His body; first on His back, and then He is turned and scourged in front. What He finds hardest is being completely deprived of His garments.

"Beneath the repeated blows, the skin first swells up and is then torn; the blood flows so that His whole body looks terrible and red with wounds and blood. When the soldiers have fully satisfied their cruelty, they untie Our Saviour and He falls down; it is a heartrending sight."

The accounts of the scourging given by Venerable Maria d'Agreda and Catherine Emmerich are more detailed than those of the above-mentioned two and, in both, a description of the instruments of torture is given. Both of these accounts agree with the account given by Teresa Neumann in saying that there were six executioners; that Our Lord's hands were bound to a ring at the top of a high pillar. Catherine Emmerich and Teresa Neumann say expressly that the Body was turned and scourged in front; Venerable Maria d'Agreda describes the striking of the face in the same way as Catherine Emmerich, which supposes that the Body was turned. Both St. Bridget and Catherine Emmerich refer to the man who came and cut the cords which bound Our Lord to the pillar, saying to the executioners that they had no right to kill an innocent man.

In describing the scourges used by the first two executioners, Catherine Emmerich says:

"The whips or scourges which they first made use of appeared to me to be made of a species of flexible white wood, or perhaps they were composed of the sinews of the ox, or of strips of leather."

While the first two executioners were engaged in scourging Our Lord, Catherine Emmerich saw the other executioners preparing new scourges:

"I saw groups of infamous young men, who were busying themselves in preparing fresh scourges, while others went to seek thorny brambles. Servants of the High Priests gave the executioners money; they had also a large jar filled with bright red liquid which inebriated them and increased their fury.

"The next two executioners made use of a species of thorny stick covered with knots and splinters. The blows of these sticks tore His flesh to pieces; His blood spouted out so as to stain their arms, and He groaned, prayed and shuddered.

"Two fresh executioners used scourges composed of small chains, or straps covered with iron hooks, which penetrated to the bone and tore off pieces of flesh at every blow.

"The executioners untied Jesus and fastened Him up with His back turned towards the pillar. They recommenced scourging Him with even greater fury than before; one among them struck Him constantly on the face with a new rod.

"I saw the Blessed Virgin in a continual ecstasy during the scourging of Her Divine Son; she saw and suffered with inexpressible love and grief all the torments He was enduring."

The description of the scourging by the Venerable Maria d'Agreda corresponds closely with that of Catherine Emmerich. As both were describing from memory what they saw, and not recording what was told to them, it is not surprising that the description by both of the scourges used is not exactly alike. The Venerable Maria d'Agreda says that some of the scourges were composed of hard knotted ropes, others of ox-sinews and others of strips of leather. The description of the mangled condition of Our Lord's body after the scourging given by all four are much alike and correspond with the evidence from the Holy Shroud. Venerable Maria d'Agreda speaks of one of the executioners striking Our Lord on the face; and of Our Lady as sharing in the physical sufferings of her Divine Son.

She concludes her moving account as follows:

"When the second pair of executioners had retired, all the veins of the most holy body were already opened and the body itself appeared like one continuous wound, so that the third pair of executioners found no sound spot in which to open further veins. Nevertheless, these commenced to scourge Him with inhuman cruelty so that the sinless, virgin body of Christ Our Lord was completely torn. Even pieces of His flesh fell to the ground and in many parts of His shoulders the bones were laid bare and became plainly visible, all covered with blood. In some places the surfaces of the bones thus laid bare was greater than the palm of the hand. In order to destroy the last traces of the peerless beauty of the Sacred Humanity, the fairest among the children of men, the

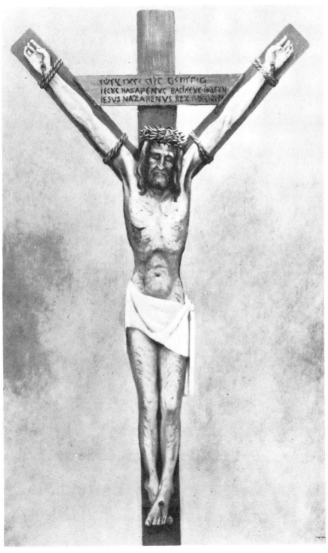

The Crucifixion according to the evidence from the Holy Shroud, and the visions of St. Bridget of Sweden and others.

The Image of the Holy Face

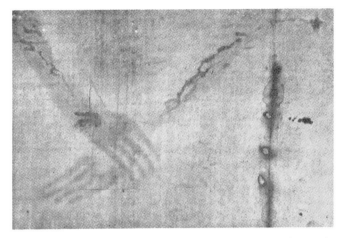

Image showing the traces of blood on both arms that flowed from the wounds of the hands.

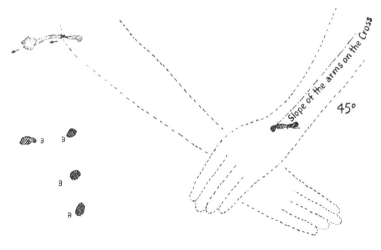

Tracing of above image made on the reverse side by Cordonnier showing the slope of Our Lord's arms when extended on the Cross (45°)

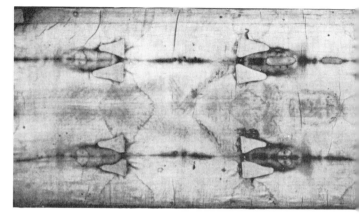

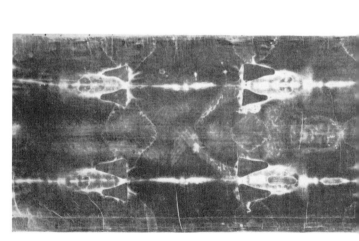

Negative and positive images showing the right leg perfectly straight, the left slightly bent and both feet pointing downwards and turned inwards.

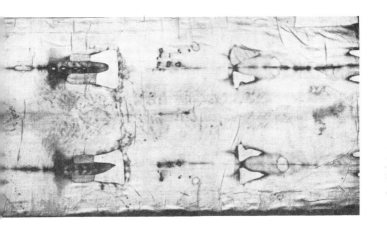

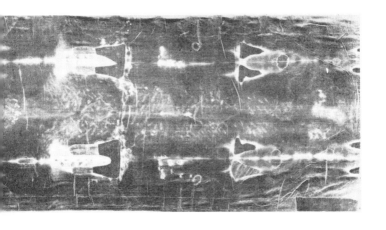

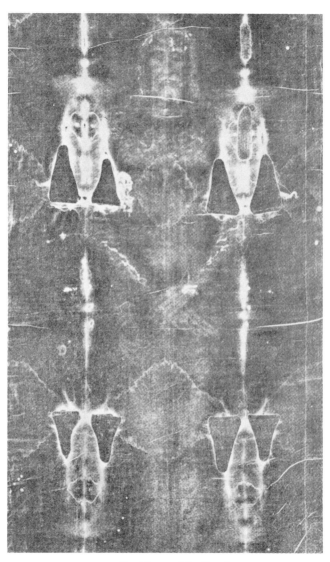

Front Image of the Shroud

Back Image of the Shroud

The Crucifix in the Church of Coesfeld

executioners struck Our Divine Saviour with their scourges on the face, the feet and the hands. No spot that their wild rage could reach was left sound and whole. The precious blood flowed down in streams to the earth and collected in pools on the ground. The adorable face of Jesus was all swollen and wounded so that His eyes were hindered from seeing by the blood and bruises with which they were covered. In addition, they covered the face with their filthy spittle which they spat upon it in derision, so that truly, 'He was glutted with reproaches.'"

The Crowning of Our Lord with Thorns

The relics of the Crown of Thorns which are still preserved add further sorrowful details to the account by the Evangelists. These relics consist of the outer frame-work into which the thorny brambles were woven and which is kept in the Cathedral of Notre Dame in Paris, and two of the thorns which are kept in the Church of the Holy Cross in Rome. These thorns are over an inch long and are very sharp. Experts say that the relics are only part of the thorn and that the whole thorn was two or three inches long. Long sharp thorns of this kind abound not only in Palestine but in tropical and semi-tropical countries.

The image on the Holy Shroud confirms the Gospel account of the Crowning with Thorns and helps to prove that the thorns preserved in the Church of the Holy Cross in Rome are genuine. Paul Vignon remarks that no ordinary thorns would have made such deep wounds as the Holy Shroud reveals; nothing less than big thorns like the relics preserved, if repeatedly struck, would account for the wounds. The marks of wounds of the head on the Holy Shroud which are not confined to the brow and the back of the head, as Cordonnier remarks, show that the actual crown of thorns was not in the form of a circlet, as it is usually represented in art, but in the form of a cap or helmet which covered the whole head. The marks of the wounds on the crown of the head are not visible because the band that passed under the chin was tied on the top of the head (as the image of the Holy Shroud shows) and prevented the Shroud from coming in contact with the top of the head. However, the rivulets of blood that flowed through the hair down the face and on the back of the head are evidence that the innumerable thorns made wounds over the whole head. On the brow there is a trace of blood in the form of the figure '3'. Various explanations are given why the blood in that case did not flow down vertically as we would expect; Vignon's explanation that the flow of the blood was impeded by the frame-work of the crown of thorns, which was tight around the head, is the most probable.

The Accounts of the Contemplatives of the Crowning with Thorns

St. Bridget of Sweden leaves us no account of the actual crowning with thorns but she tells us that when the crucifixion was completed, the crown of thorns was again placed on Our Lord's head:

"This done, they replaced on His head the crown of thorns which they had taken off while affixing Him to the cross, and fastened it on His most sacred head. It so wounded His venerable head that His eyes were filled with the blood that flowed down." (Rev. Bk. VII.)

The Venerable Maria d'Agreda sees the Crowning with Thorns in her vision as follows:

"The executioners brought Our Saviour to the guardhouse, where they again stripped Him of His clothes in a most cruel and insulting manner. They put upon His shoulders a dirty torn purple mantle in order that thus clad as a mock king He may serve as an object of mockery and derision for them. On His sacred head they placed a network woven with thorns to represent a crown. This network was composed of big strong thorns with very sharp points and was pressed down with such force that many of the thorns pierced the skull. The pain from the crowning with thorns was one of the greatest that the Son of God suffered in His Passion."

The account continues and tells how the whole cohort of Roman soldiers then came and took part in the cruel mockery.

The accounts of Catherine Emmerich and Teresa Neumann, while corresponding with the Gospel account, add many details. The account of Catherine Emmerich is as follows:

"The executioners were about fifty in number, mostly slaves or servants of the jailers and soldiers. A mob that gathered round the building was displaced by a thousand Roman soldiers who were drawn up in order and stationed there. The executioners tore off the garments of Jesus thereby re-opening all His wounds. They threw over His shoulders an old scarlet mantle. They dragged Him to the seat prepared, having first placed the crown of thorns on His head. The crown of thorns was made of three branches plaited together, the greatest part of the thorns being purposely turned inwards so as to pierce Our Lord's head. Having first placed these twisted branches on His forehead, they tied them tightly together at the back of His head ... They put a reed in His hand. They then seized the reed from His hand and struck His head so violently that His eyes were filled with blood; they knelt before Him; derided Him; spat in His face and buffeted Him, saying at the same time, 'Hail, King of the Jews!'"

The following is Teresa Neumann's account of the crowning with thorns:

"The crown of thorns which is now ready is placed on Our Lord's head like a helmet; it is not just a crown as we see it depicted in our pictures. One of the soldiers presses the crown of thorns firmly on His head. The blood flows down His whole face which shows signs of intense pain during this terrible treatment.

"Then the executioners put something like a staff in the hands of our dear Saviour, on the upper end of which is a natural knob, very much like a corn cob, like those I have seen at Fockenfeld, only smaller.

"They now amuse themselves with it, making mock genuflections before Him. I was specially indignant about the contempt implied by this mockery of bowing the knee before Our Saviour. They spit in His face and give themselves up to uncontrollable laughter over the defencelessness of the prisoner.

"Our Saviour often opens His mouth as if to get more air and as if He is thirsty. At this, one of them spits directly into His mouth; this form of insult deeply grieves our Divine Saviour."

The Evidence from the Holy Shroud

The best commentators on the Holy Shroud, including Paul Vignon, Dr. Barbet and Judica-Cordiglia are agreed that both the Holy Shroud and the Holy Tunic of Argenteuil provide certain evidence that Our Saviour carried a rough, heavy object on His right shoulder.

The following is Professor Judica-Cordiglia's description of the wound on Our Lord's shoulder as seen on the Holy Shroud:

"In the outer third of the region above the right shoulder-blade there is a very large contusion, approximately 10 cm. by 9 cm. It is made of abrasions of various sizes and shapes one over another. It shows indistinctly the blows of the scourging, but more clearly than these the trace of a heavy, rigid yet shifting object, whose movements compressed and opened the former abrasions. *This load was the Cross.* The left shoulder shows no sign of having borne a heavy load."

The Accounts of the Contemplatives of the Carrying of the Cross

The description of Our Lord's sufferings on the Sorrowful Way was given to St. Bridget by Our Blessed Lady; it is as follows:

"And when He was condemned, they gave Him His cross to bear. And when He had carried it a short way, one came up and assumed it. Meanwhile as my Son was going to the place of His Passion, some smote Him on the back, others struck Him in the face, so violently that, though I did not see the person striking, I distinctly heard the sound of the blow." (Rev. Bk. I.)

The Venerable Maria d'Agreda gives a long account of the way to Calvary and, as is her wont, she gives the prayer Our Lord offered to His Heavenly Father when taking up His cross. According to her account, the beams of the cross were roughly hewn and were of very heavy wood. Our Lord's hands were untied so that He could hold the cross which they placed on His wounded shoulder. As in Teresa Neumann's account, ropes were attached to His Body by which those in front pulled Him forward to hasten His steps and those behind at times held Him back to vex and torment Him. In this cruel manner they thus led Him along so that with the heavy weight on His shoulder He staggered from side to side and fell to the ground several times. As the streets were paved with rough stones, new wounds were caused, especially to His knees. Here it may be remarked that during the vision of the carrying of the cross wounds appear on Teresa Neumann's knees which bleed profusely. As Our Lord staggers along, the cross on His shoulder sways and often hits against the crown of thorns and embeds it more deeply in His sacred head.

Our Blessed Lady, in the company of St. John and the holy women, followed her Divine Son on the way to Calvary. When prevented from approaching Him by the surging crowd, an angel guided the little company through a side-street, and Mother and Son met face to face. She fell on her knees and adored Him with deepest veneration but was rudely pushed aside by the executioners and the sad procession moved on. At her earnest prayer the Heavenly Father permitted that the heavy load of the cross be lightened, and Simon of Cyrene was constrained to help Him to carry it.

Catherine Emmerich's account of the carrying of the cross is again the most detailed of any account that we have. It agrees with Teresa Neumann's account in all details and refers to Our Lord's prayer when He received the cross, which Maria d'Agreda gives. In her account, the cross consists of three parts, the central beam and two cross-bars. These were tied together at the court of Pilate and placed on Our Lord's right shoulder. Like Maria d'Agreda, she says that Our Lord's hands were loose and that He held the cross on His shoulder with His right hand. In agreement with both Maria d'Agreda and Teresa Neumann, she says that ropes were attached to a belt round Our Lord's waist and were held by two men in front and two behind. Those in front dragged Him forward to hasten His steps and those behind held Him back with the result that He fell several times. Agreeing again with Teresa Neumann, she says that Our Lord fell not merely three, but several times. She describes in detail five of these falls, the first of which was caused by a large stone across a dirty part of the street that was used as a stepping-stone. There is a slight apparent contradiction in her account. In describing the crucifixion, she tells how the crown of thorns which He wore had to be removed in order to take off the seamless robe, thus showing that He wore the crown of thorns on the way to Calvary; but in her account of the carrying of the cross she had said that the boy who carried the title carried also the crown of thorns. A possible explanation is that the crown of thorns had been removed when Our Lord was putting on His own clothes after the condemnation by Pilate and had been held by the boy who carried the title, and that it had been replaced on His head when He had put on His clothes.

The following is Teresa Neumann's account of the Way of the Cross:

"The Way of the Cross as I see it in vision differs considerably from the Way of the Cross as we make it in church. Our Divine Lord has a leathern girdle round His body. Cords are fastened to this and He is led by them. He is dragged forward by means of these cords. He wears a reddish-brown tunic, which reaches to His ankles. He does not wear a cloak.

"I see the meeting of Jesus with His Mother every Friday. Jesus says something to her but very briefly. It is just a few words of greeting. The Mother of God wears a bluish-grey, long cloak. She has a veil thrown over her head. It is of coarser material than our veils. Mary is accompanied by several women, and by St. John. He is the only man among the attendants of the Mother of the Lord. He is young, younger than our Saviour, with no beard but long hair. Of course, I do not hear St. John called by his name, but from his appearance and bearing, I think it cannot be anyone else but him.

"The crowd pressing behind brings the meeting of Jesus with His Mother quickly to an end, and the procession moves on. In the crush, Jesus falls. His Mother sees Him fall. The people have no pity for Jesus.

"When our Saviour falls, there is a short halt. Meanwhile,

those who hold Jesus look around them and come upon Simon of Cyrene, whom they regard as one who hitherto has taken no part against Jesus and who will the more easily be forced to the contemptible task than the others who, on the way of the cross, are filled with hatred for Jesus. Simon comes up with three boys, not actually in the procession, but I see him come from the side. He really wants to pass on. He would prefer to refuse the service, but they constrain him. He resists but has to yield. Later, he has compassion on Jesus and tries vigorously to lighten Our Lord's burden—I call him 'Simon' only because he is thus named in the devotion of the Stations of the Cross.

"The cross Jesus carries has not the form we know. It is really no cross but only the beams for one. The shorter of these are tied to the longer.

"Veronica takes the cloth she offers Our Lord on the Way of the Cross from her left shoulder. Jesus presses it to His face. He cannot be said to wipe it. Whether He does this because wiping His face would make the wounds smart, or because the fine cloth might be entangled in the thorns, I do not know. When Veronica's cloth is returned to her, I see that It bears traces like stars, of the blood of Jesus. She does not get it back as it was. The whole face of Jesus is covered with blood. His beard is moistened with blood and His eyes full of blood. Veronica hides the cloth at once under her garments.

"After the meeting with Veronica, Our Lord goes forward with difficulty and the shouting mob thrusts Veronica back. The holy women of Jerusalem, as they are generally called, are many—a whole crowd. They stay on one side and let our Saviour pass them by. They have small children with them, whose mothers point out Our Lord to them. As He passes, Our dear Lord says something to them. When He reaches the place of execution, He again falls to the ground at the foot of the hill where He is to be crucified. Actually He has fallen, or at least stumbled, not merely three, but many times.

"I do not see how the cross is made, because while the final preparations for the execution are being made, Our Lord is led away. Jesus sits on a stone waiting to be fetched, lost in prayer. His hands are not folded but He repeatedly wrings them, looks up to heaven several times and then again He lowers His head and looks at the ground. Thus He is quite lost in Himself."

(The completed Cross, according to Teresa's visions, consisted of *three,* not two, beams. The beams for the arms rose slanting upward. It was a Cross divided so as to form the letter Y, like the Cross on the Gothic Chasuble.

The Evidence of the Holy Shroud about the Manner in Which Our Lord Was Crucified

As already mentioned, the evidence from the Holy Shroud on the crucifixion must be accepted, as on the other physical sufferings of Our Lord, in preference to conjectures based on books about Roman antiquities. The chief points of the evidence of the Shroud about the crucifixion are:—(1) that three nails, not four, were used; (2) that the right foot was next to the Cross and the left foot over it; (3) that the nails were driven in the part of the hand near the wrist. As only the back of the hand can be seen on the image, the Shroud cannot be said to tell us at what point exactly the nail entered the front of the hand; (4) that there is indication of the angle that Our Lord's arms made with the horizontal; (5) that *Rigor Mortis* had set in before Our Lord was taken down from the Cross; (6) that the limbs were stretched violently before the feet were nailed.

With regard to the first and second point, all the commentators of the Holy Shroud are agreed that there is conclusive evidence from the image on it that only three nails were used, and that the right foot was next to the Cross. On the image, the right leg appears stretched out straight, with the foot pointing downwards and turned inwards; the left leg appears to be a few inches shorter, the knee is slightly bent and the foot is turned inwards behind the right so that the image of it from the instep to the toes does not appear.

With regard to the wounds made by the nails on Our Lord's hands, we have only the image of the wound on the back of the left hand, because the left hand was placed over the right and prevented the image of the right hand from being record-ed on the Shroud. The image of the left hand shows that the nail was driven through the bony part, or the heel, of the hand called the carpus, and not through the wrist (as claimed by Dr. Barbet), or through the palm.

The position of the legs and feet, as shown on the Shroud, with the right leg stretched out straight, the left knee slightly bent and the feet crossed shows that the *Rigor Mortis* had set in before Our Lord's Body was taken down from the Cross; there are other signs besides.

It is quite clear from the image on the Shroud that the right leg was stretched out straight, and that the left knee was slightly bent because the left foot was nailed on top of the right. Dr. Barbet proved unintentionally by the experiment of nailing a corpse to a cross that this could only happen if the limbs had been stretched before the feet were nailed. He nailed the corpse to a cross placed on the ground and found (1) that he could not nail the right foot flat against the cross, as the Shroud shows Our Lord's feet to have been nailed, without bending the right knee slightly and the left knee still more, (2) that when he raised the cross, the weight of the body stretched the arms by 5 cm. and brought the body down till the arms made an angle of 65° with the perpendicular and

25° with the horizontal, and, (3) that the knees bent correspondingly and receded from the cross. However, from the image on the Shroud, it is quite clear that the right leg is perfectly straight, that the right foot points downwards as if the body stood on its toes, and that the left knee is only slightly bent. Dr. Barbet, therefore, unintentionally proved that the crucifixion of Our Lord was not done in the same way as he crucified the corpse.

Anne Catherine Emmerich's account of her vision of the crucifixion explains clearly why the right leg is perfectly straight and why the foot points downwards as if it had been nailed flat against the Cross. In her account of her vision, she says that the executioners first placed the Body of Our Lord on the Cross and marked the places for the nails both for hands and feet, and that they deliberately marked them too far apart. They then made a cavity in the upright beam for the heel and then fixed a small piece of wood on the upright beam for the instep of the foot, in which they bored a hole to receive the nail that pierced the feet. When they had nailed Our Lord's hands, the feet did not reach down to the place prepared for them, and so they attached ropes to the ankles and pulled them down with all their strength.

As we shall see later on, St. Bridget of Sweden, Venerable Maria d'Agreda and Teresa Neumann describe the crucifixion of Our Lord in exactly the same way, except they do not mention the small detail of making a cavity in the upright beam for the heel to fit into, so that it would not be necessary to bend the right knee.

Dr. Barbet nailed both the hands and feet to the cross while it was on the ground; if he had nailed only the hands to the cross-beam and raised the corpse on to the top of the upright beam before nailing the feet, it is true that the weight of the body would have stretched the arms by 5 cm.

but it would not have stretched the legs also; and if a cavity had not been made for the heel, it would have been necessary to bend the knees.

Dr. Barbet calculated by how much the arms would have been stretched if the Body of Our Lord sank down till the arms made an angle of 45° instead of 65° with the perpendicular, and found that the amount would be 22 cm. (over 7 inches) and as it would be impossible to stretch the arms by 22 cm. he concluded that the angle which Our Lord's arms made with the perpendicular could not have been 45°. He examined a photograph of the Holy Shroud and believed that he had found evidence from the trace of blood on the back of Our Lord's left hand that the angle was actually 65°.

Commentators on the Holy Shroud, with the exception of Engineer Cordonnier, have accepted Dr. Barbet's figure without question. Engineer Cordonnier, however, gives the angle as 45° in number V of his illustrations given with his book *Le Christ Dans Sa Passion Revele Par Le Saint Suaire De Turin.* Cordonnier's difference about the angle with Dr. Barbet escaped notice because he did not mention the degree of the angle in the book itself, but just referred the reader to No. V illustration (2. V.) on which he makes the angle 45°.

A glance at a photograph of the Shroud will show that Our Lord's wrists were bent sideways (thus lessening the appearance of the angle by 20°) at the time of the burial to make the hands meet in front of the Body. Cordonnier evidently took this bend into account when calculating the angle, and Dr. Barbet did not. When Our Lord hung on the Cross, the joint of the wrist could not have been bent sideways, as it appears in the image of the Shroud, for the nail was driven through the bony part of the hand and not through the wrist.

The angle which Our Lord's arms made both with the perpendicular and the horizontal was, therefore, 45°, as Cordonnier makes it.

When making his experiment, Dr. Barbet used the common form of the Latin cross, and presumed rightly that at the crucifixion of Our Lord, His arms were extended horizontally. In that case, it would have been impossible for the Body to sink down till the arms made an angle of 45° with the crossbeam, for it would require a stretching of Our Lord's arms by 22 cm. But as the contemplatives saw the crucifixion, it was not the common form of the Cross that was used but the form that appears on the Gothic chasuble with its arms pointing upwards. When Our Lord's hands were being nailed, the arms were stretched upwards, and when they were nailed it was found that the feet did not reach down to the place prepared for them and so the executioners pulled them down violently.

Fr. Gallwey S.J., in *The Watches of the Passion* summarizes the accounts of the crucifixion found in the visions of St. Bridget of Sweden and Anne Catherine Emmerich as follows:

"The holes for the nails are designed too far apart; but what matters that? His limbs can be stretched. . . In that hour the Saviour is not ignorant of the boast that a persecuting judge shall one day utter over the racked martyr, 'I have made him a foot longer than God made him.' He wishes to taste the chalice of His martyrs and to bless it. . .

"The most troublesome part of the work is now to come. The ropes and chains which had been used to bind Our Saviour must now help to stretch His sacred body . . . Some of the executioners throw their weight on the wounded limbs to prevent the sacred hands from being torn from their places. The others pull, and rack, and dislocate the joints till they have forced the feet to their proper position and there bind them with ropes, and nail them to the Cross."

41

The Evidence from the Holy Shroud for the Form of the Cross

Experts on the Holy Shroud are agreed about two facts which, once pointed out, can be observed by anyone. The first fact is that there is a trace of blood along both arms of Our Lord from the wound in the hand towards the shoulder, not made by any wound on the arms but caused by the flow of blood along the arms from the wounds in the hands. This flow of blood could only have run along the arms if they were tight against the cross-bars thus forming a sort of furrow, and had remained so until the death of Christ.

The second fact is that there is another trace of blood on the back of Our Lord's left hand (the right hand is hidden under the left) where a little of the blood from the wound in the hand trickled down between the hand and the wood of the Cross. As this blood dripped down vertically, it gives the angle which Our Lord's arms made with that line—or what amounts to the same thing—the angle which the arms made with the horizontal and the perpendicular. As already mentioned, Dr. Barbet found that the arms of the corpse that he nailed to a cross were dragged down by the weight of the body to an angle of 25° with the horizontal, or 65° with the perpendicular. He then examined the image on the Shroud and thought that the mark on the back of the hand showed the angle made by Our Lord's arms to this mark (or to the perpendicular) to be also 65° (or 25° to the horizontal). He failed to observe that the joint of the wrist had been bent sideways at the burial, thus lessening the angle by about 20°. It did not occur to him that there were other factors besides the weight of the body to account for the position of the arms: the form of the Cross, the fact that the limbs had been stretched.

Engineer Cordonnier, another of the experts on the Shroud,

just gives a drawing of the angle among his illustrations and makes it about 45°. Anyone can see how Dr. Barbet made the mistake, by not taking the bend of the wrist into consideration. Even if the angle had been 25° with the horizontal, as Dr. Barbet thought, the arms of Our Lord could not have been tight enough to the Cross to prevent the blood from flowing down to the ground before it reached the elbow, unless the arms of the Cross sloped upwards at the same angle as the arms of Our Lord. It is quite clear, however, that the angle given by Cordonnier is the right one; a glance at the illustration will convince anyone of the fact.

Engineer Cordonnier's keen eye noticed another fact that helps to prove that Our Lord's limbs were stretched before the feet were nailed. On page 11 of his little book he writes: "The arms (of Our Lord) appear to be very long; it seems that Christ had been almost pulled asunder (*ecartele)* on the Cross, so much so that when the nails were removed, His arms hang down unsustained by the enfeebled shoulders."

Cordonnier's evidence from the Holy Shroud about the angle at which Our Lord hung on the Cross and the fact that the arms appear to have been torn from their sockets (which the mere weight of the Body would not have effected) is all the more valuable because he was not trying to establish any theory; he was just giving the facts that the Holy Shroud revealed.

We conclude, therefore, that these two traces of blood on Our Lord's arms, about which the experts are agreed, can be explained only by the form of the Cross that appears on the Gothic chasuble. Furthermore, the arms of Our Lord must have remained tightly pressed to the Cross for the whole time that He hung on it, otherwise the blood would have dripped down at the point where they parted from the Cross. In practice, this could only have happened if the arms were tied to the Cross. This is how the crucifixion was seen by Catherine Emmerich and Teresa Neumann. Catherine Emmerich says that there was a rope tied round Our Lord's wrists binding them to the Cross and another round His chest and that some of the ropes were removed when the Cross was raised. Teresa Neumann says that the arms of the Cross slanted upwards and that each of Our Lord's arms was tied to it in two places: at the wrists and at the arm-pits. St. Bridget saw the Cross with its arms slanting upwards and the arms of Our Lord fitting to the Cross.

The mode of crucifixion in which the limbs are violently strained as on the rack accounts for the early death of Our Lord on the Cross. His early death has been attributed to the severity of the scourging and His other sufferings. These explain it in part only; Pilate, who saw the pitiable condition to which Christ had been reduced, wondered that He had died so soon. The fact that He was not only crucified but racked at the same time most certainly hastened His death, for Dr. Barbet tells us that the cause of death, when it came to Him, was asphyxiation due to the great difficulty of breathing. Dr. P. J. Smith claims that Dr. Barbet shows that there is overwhelming evidence that Christ died from heart failure due to extreme shock caused by exhaustion, pain and loss of blood. (The actual time that Our Lord lived on the Cross under the terrible strain was only three hours compared to three days that many of the crucified victims survived.)

Besides, Our Divine Lord Himself knew that, as He, the real Paschal Lamb, was to be sacrificed on the Festival of the Pasch, His death would have been hastened in order that His Body should be removed before sunset. He wished to suffer all the pains of crucifixion and die from them; He chose, therefore, that most painful form of crucifixion which combined the pains of crucifixion and the torture of the rack. This thought should make the holy Cross, on which He suffered so much, doubly venerable in our eyes.

Let us now see how each of the four whose visions we have been considering describes the crucifixion:

The Revelations of St. Bridget of Sweden

In Book I of the revelations of St. Bridget we read:

"Then the cruel executioners seized Him and stretched Him on the Cross. First they fixed His right hand to the beam which was pierced for the nails, and they transfixed His hand *in the part where the bone is firmest.* Then drawing the other hand with a rope, they affixed it in like manner. Then *they crucified His right foot and, over it, the left* (with two nails). This done, they fitted the crown of thorns to His head. . . . *His hands and feet were stretched most rigidly, drawn and framed to the form of the Cross.* His beard and hair all clotted with blood. . . ." (Rev. Bk. I.)

In Book IV, we read:

"Now the Cross was planted and its arms raised, so that the junction of the Cross was between shoulders, the Cross affording no support for the head, and the inscription-board was fixed to the two arms rising above the head. . . ."

In the description of the taking down from the Cross, we find the following reference to the *Rigor Mortis:*

"But now I (Our Blessed Lady) was consoled that I could touch His Body taken down from the Cross and receive Him in my bosom, examine His wounds and wipe away the blood. Then my fingers closed His mouth and I also composed His eyes; but I could not bend His stiffening arms so as to cross them on His breast. . . ." (Bk. IV.)

And in Book VII we read:

"And, opening His right hand, He laid it on the Cross, which His cruel torturers barbarously crucified, driving the nail through the part where the bone was most solid. Then violently drawing His left hand with a rope, they affixed it to the Cross in a similar manner. Then, stretching His Body beyond all bounds, they fastened His *joined feet* to the Cross, and so violently extended those glorious limbs on the Cross that all the nerves and veins were fairly broken." (Bk. VII.)

From these three accounts it is clear that the limbs of Our Lord were violently extended before being nailed; that the arms of the Cross sloped upwards; and that the *Rigor Mortis* had set in before Our Lord was taken down from the Cross.

The Venerable Maria d'Agreda tells us in her account of the crucifixion how the sacrifice demanded of Abraham to yield his father's rights over his only son to Almighty God was also demanded of Our Lady, and that she complied with the divine wish and united her share in the Passion with the sufferings of her Divine Son. She tells also how Our Blessed Lady's earnest wish was granted that she might share in all the sufferings of her Divine Son and feel in her sinless body the torments He suffered on the Cross. Of the actual crucifixion she speaks as follows:

"Then the executioners ordered the Saviour to stretch Himself on the Cross in order that they might mark the places where the holes were to be bored for the nails. The Saviour obeyed without a murmur, but the wicked men did not make the marks for the holes in the places corresponding with the dimensions of His Body but wider asunder in order to inflict upon Him a new and unheard of martyrdom. When the holes for the nails had been bored, the executioners ordered Him a second time to stretch Himself on the Cross in order that they might nail Him to it. The Saviour obeyed; He laid Himself on the Cross, stretched out His hands on that hallowed wood as the executioners had demanded.

"Immediately, one of the executioners seized His hand and

pressed it down on the hole in the arm of the Cross while another executioner took a big nail with rough edges and with a hammer drove it through the Saviour's hand and nailed it to the Cross. As the executioners through wickedness had made the holes too wide asunder, the left hand did not reach the hole prepared for it, and so the executioners fastened a chain to His hand and pulled the other end with unheard-of cruelty until the hand reached the place prepared; they then nailed it to the arm of the Cross. When this was done they took the feet, placed them one over the other, attached a rope to them, pulled them down with all their might and, with a third nail that was larger than the others, nailed both of them at the same time.

"So was that sacred Body that was united to the Godhead fastened with nails to the Cross. All its members that had been miraculously formed by the Holy Ghost were distorted and rent asunder so that all the bones thus wrenched from their sockets could be numbered."

The account of the crucifixion and of the three hours' agony on the Cross which Catherine Emmerich gives is again by far the most detailed of all the accounts we have. It agrees perfectly with Teresa Neumann's account. The following are a few quotations from it:

"When the executioners found it was impossible to drag the woolen garment which His Mother had woven for Him over His head, on account of the crown of thorns, they tore off this most painful crown, thus reopening every wound. . . . He shook like the aspen as He stood before them. . . . He was covered with open wounds and His shoulders and back were torn to the bone by the dreadful scourging He had endured. As He was unable to stand, they led Him to a large stone and placed Him roughly down upon it, but no sooner was He seated than they aggravated His sufferings by putting the crown of thorns on His head. . . . Then seizing His right arm, they dragged it to the hole prepared for the nail, and having tied it tightly down with a cord, one of them knelt on His sacred chest, a second held His hand flat and a third, taking a long thick nail, pressed it on the open palm of that adorable hand . . . . and with a great iron hammer drove it through the flesh, and far into the wood of the Cross. . . . When the executioners perceived that His left hand did not reach the hole that they had bored for the nail, they tied ropes to His left arm and pulled the left hand violently until it reached the place prepared for it. They again knelt on Him, tied down His arms and drove the second nail into His left hand. . . .

"The executioners had fastened a piece of wood at the lower part of the Cross under where the feet of Jesus were to be nailed. A hole had been pierced in this wood to receive the nail when driven through His feet, and there was likewise a little hollow place for the heels. The whole Body of Our Lord had been dragged up and contracted by the violent manner in which the executioners had stretched out His arms. Perceiving that His feet did not reach the bit of wood placed for them . . . they fastened a rope to His right leg and dragged it violently until it reached this bit of wood and then tied it down as tightly as possible. The agony which Jesus suffered was indescribable. . . . They then fastened His left foot to His right and, having first bored a hole through them with a sort of piercer, they took a very long nail·and drove it completely through both feet into the Cross below. . . . During the whole time of the crucifixion, Our Lord never ceased praying and repeating those passages of the Psalms that He was then accomplishing. . . .

". . . . The eminence on which the Cross was planted was about two feet higher than the surrounding parts; the feet of Jesus were sufficiently near to the ground for His friends to be able to reach to kiss them and His face was turned to the north-west."

It was customary for critics to dismiss Catherine Emmerich's account of the crucifixion with the remark that she naturally saw the crucifixion as it was represented on the cross in the church of her native Coesfeld. In fact, in a booklet on that famous cross, the author tries to show by quoting only the first half of her description of the crucifixion, that she saw it just as represented on that cross. She says that, when the left hand was pulled to the place prepared for it and nailed, the arms of Our Lord no longer fitted to the arms of the Cross which sloped upwards; but in the second part of her description she says that the executioners pulled the Body of Our Lord down so as to make them fit. The appearance of Our Lord on the Cross when the crucifixion was completed was therefore so much different from the appearance of the Coesfeld crucifix, that she could not have gotten her idea from it. Besides, St. Bridget, who lived before the crucifix of Coesfeld was made, gives the same description of the crucifixion as Catherine Emmerich. It is quite possible that the idea of both the Cross of Coesfeld and of the Cross on the Gothic chasuble was taken from the account given in the visions of St. Bridget. The evidence from the Holy Shroud confirms the whole four accounts of the crucifixion given above.

The united testimony of all five goes to show that the sufferings of Our Lord in His Passion, and especially on the Cross, were far greater than we have been accustomed to picture to ourselves from the reading of pious books about the Passion.

Teresa Neumann's account of the crucifixion is as follows:

"Before beginning to crucify Him, the soldiers offer Our Saviour something to drink, but He does not drink it. They cannot take off His long tunic while He is wearing the crown of thorns. This, therefore, is removed. But this is not easy, and it sticks fast in His sacred head on account of the many thorns. Afterwards it is put on again. Meanwhile, the blood streams over His whole face. Our Saviour wears a cloth round His loins.

"When He is stripped of His garments, I am painfully struck with the large deep wound on the right shoulder from the carrying of the Cross. I feel special compassion with Jesus for this in that I have, either during the vision or after it, a similar special pain.

"Our Lord is nailed to the Cross as it lies on the ground. He first has to place Himself on the Cross and stretch Himself out. His hands are wound round with cords by which they are then held fast. First the right hand is nailed. When the left hand is about to be nailed, I see the men held up in their work. They cannot drive the nail in at once. I think the reason for this is that the holes for the nails had been bored beforehand and it now appears that they had been bored too far apart. So one of the executioners violently pulls the left hand of Jesus by the rope while another kneels on the breast of Our dear Saviour to prevent the Body from being pulled out of the centre. Finally, one of the executioners places a nail on the left hand and drives it through into the wood. During the nailing, clear blood begins to flow at once from the wounds.

"When, with heavy blows of the hammer, the nails are driven through the living hands, the harsh sound of the sharp hammer-blows goes through my very bones and pierces my soul. As I am in a fainting condition at beholding how the nails press through the hands and feet of Jesus, I cannot describe this pain nor compare it with anything. It is not as if the nails pierce my own hands and feet. I can think very little about myself, for my whole attention is directed alone to Our dear Saviour.

"When His hands have been nailed, Our Saviour raises His two feet trembling, for He writhes under the pain. And in order that His feet may be nailed too, they are wound round with cords and one of the executioners drags them down with great violence. The feet are first tied and then one nail is driven through them both. A small piece of wood for the feet is fixed to the Cross. When all is ready, the Cross is raised. This sight means terrible suffering for me. Thus, Our dear Saviour hangs there in the sight of all."

"When the time comes for Him to speak to Her and to St. John, He first turns to Mary on His right side, but with only a few words, which, of course, I do not understand. Then Jesus turns to John on the other side. John now goes to Mary and holds her by the arm to give her some support. The face of the Mother of God is wan and white as if she felt ill.

"The Cross on which Jesus hangs is quite low. I hear Him speaking from the Cross, but I do not understand the language, I do not know what language. It is not Latin.

"The inscription on the Cross above the head of Jesus comprises three lines of different writing. On the Way of the Cross, the tablet was carried in front by a lad. The first line does not look like letters; they are only scratches. Only the second line really looks like letters. In front of the Cross near the tunic of Jesus sit some men who throw three small four-sided pieces with black spots, (dice). I do not know what they are doing. Our Saviour looks down at them and says something. Behind Jesus, into Whose face I look, I see many, many houses. What is most wonderful about these houses is that they have no roof and no gable. They look as if they had been cut out flat. Not long after the Cross is raised up, the sky becomes more and more overcast. Yet it is not so dark but that Our dear Saviour can still be seen. This darkness makes a terrible and frightening impression on me.

"Our dear Saviour becomes visibly weaker. Then He opens His mouth and lets His tongue be seen for a long time. He also says something. One of the soldiers has a sponge on a rather short stick which he dips into a vessel near the soldiers who stand by in a group. Then one of the soldiers steps up to Jesus with the wet sponge and holds the sponge before His mouth. I do not see if Jesus takes any of it.

"The weakness of Jesus increases more and more. Our dear Saviour raises His head and says a few words in a feeble voice. . . . Moreover, He cannot really raise His head properly because the crown of thorns prevents Him. The whole time so far He has not been able to lean His head against the Cross because of this.

"One can see how the end draws nearer and nearer. His whole Body begins to look bluish, His eyes sink deeper into their sockets, His face and nose become pointed and drawn, and the color of His face almost yellowish-grey.

"After a while, Jesus suddenly raises His head as much as He can, as if He wishes to rouse Himself, and, looking upwards, calls out something in a loud voice. Then He bows His head. His knees give way. Our dear Saviour sinks down on the Cross. *He is dead.* His head falls slowly on His breast."

The Opening of Our Lord's Side

In St. John's Gospel we read:

"But one of the soldiers with a spear opened His side: and immediately there came forth blood and water." (John, XIX, 34.)

The imprint of the wound made by the lance is plainly visible on the Holy Shroud showing that the lance had entered between the fifth and sixth ribs on the right side. Under this wound there is a broad trace of dark, thick blood down the front of the body which indicates that Our Lord's side had been pierced as He hung on the Cross. The blood was dark and thick and coagulated on the chest, showing patches formed by some colorless liquid—the water mentioned by St. John. Both Anne Catherine Emmerich and Teresa Neumann in their visions see this wound being made by a Roman soldier on horse-back who drives his lance against the right side of Our Lord's Body with such force that its point appears on the back.

Anne Catherine Emmerich's description of the piercing of Our Lord's side is as follows:

"The officer seized his lance and rode up to the mound where the Cross was planted and taking his lance in both hands, thrust it so completely into the right side of Jesus that the point went through the heart, and appeared on the left side."

Teresa Neumann also in her vision sees the officer ride up the mound on horse-back, and of the piercing of the side she says:

"When the sacred side of Jesus is transpierced with the lance, I see that the lance is vigorously thrust through the right side opposite the heart. The lance comes out on the other side, but only a little shows. I do not see the two thieves."

Some of the Fathers also say that the point of the lance appeared on the back. On the Holy Shroud there is the mark of a wound on the left side of the back at the point where Catherine Emmerich and Teresa Neumann say that the lance emerged. This wound would account for the trace of blood across the small of the back. It is hard to see why blood should have flowed out from the wound in front when the Body of Our Lord was placed on its back, but it is quite natural to suppose that it came from the wound on the back.

In Teresa Neumann's stigmata the wound on the side seems

to go right through her heart, and it appears on her back like the point of a lance.

APPENDIX
Answer to Common Queries

Dr. Barbet in his book *A Doctor At Calvary* states that he amputated an arm two-thirds of the way up from a vigorous man. He then drove a square nail of about ⅓ of an inch (a copy of the nail of the Passion) into the middle of the palm, in the third space. He gently suspended a weight of 88 pounds from the elbow (half the weight of the body of a man about 6 feet tall—the weight of the Body of Christ on the Cross was about 176 pounds). He then gave the whole a moderate shake and he saw the nail suddenly forcing its way through the hand.

He further states that it was not a weight of 88 pounds but nearly 209 pounds, which was dragging on each nail in the hands of the Crucified, for, as we know, the division of a weight between two oblique and symmetrical forces means that each one is bearing considerably more than half the weight.

We hold with consulted surgeons that if Dr. Barbet put a 209 pound weight instead of 88 pounds on the amputated arm and if he drove the nail into the wrist as is shown in the X-ray picture of his book *A Doctor At Calvary* the whole hand would be pulled off with such a weight if the amputated arm was not tied down near the wrist and the elbow.

STIGMATIZED PALMS

It is certain that most stigmatists like St. Francis of Assisi, Padre Pio, Teresa Neumann, etc., have their wounds in the palms of their hands. This does not signify that these stigmata are the exact reproduction of the wounds in the hands of Our Saviour. These wounds vary in appearance, and they are more or less superficial or deep, varying from excoriation to a gaping hole. Passerini's edition of *Fioretti* p. 170 says of St. Francis: "And thus his hands and feet appeared nailed with nails, of which the heads were in the palms of the hands and in the *soles* of the feet, outside the flesh. Their points came out on the back of the hands and the feet, where they were twisted and turned back; this was done in such a way that it would have been possible to pass a finger quite easily, as through a ring, where this twisting and turning back had taken place, for it came out right above the flesh. And the heads of the nails were round and black." And elsewhere he says that these nail formations could be moved in the grooves where they were lodged through the hands and feet. This was definitely learned after his death. Certainly these stigmata are not the exact reproduction of the wounds of Our Saviour when He was laid in the shroud. The heads of the nails in the soles of St. Francis feet is the reverse of what happened to Jesus.

The stigmatists may have mental aberrations regarding the real stigmatization of Jesus and their wounds may have only a mystical value for themselves. Teresa Neumann said to one of her friends; "Do not think that Our Saviour was nailed in the hands, where I have my stigmata. These marks have only a mystical meaning. Jesus must have been fixed more firmly on the Cross." The revelation of the Blessed Virgin to St. Bridget of Sweden (Bk. I, c. 10) says; "My Son's hands were pierced at the spot where the bone was most solid."

BLOOD AND WATER

"But one of the soldiers with a spear opened His side, and immediately there came out blood and water." (Jn. XIX 34.)

Origen and many of the early writers considered this *mir-*

aculous. Recent autopsies show that the blow of the lance which was given to the right side reached the right auricle of the heart, perforating the pericardium which is a sac containing a watery fluid or serum (hydropericardium). Dr. Judica, in his article in *Medicina Italiana* (Milan, 1937), found, in experimenting, that blood came from the right auricle and the water from the pericardium. He holds that there was a "serous traumatic pericarditis," brought on by the blows and the cudgelling, and the terrible scourging in which the chest was injured. Such violence would produce a rapid and abundant serous discharge.

The Opening of Our Lord's Side

In most, if not all books on the Shroud, the explanation of the trace of blood across the loins is that it flowed from the wound made by the lance in front. This does not explain this trace satisfactorily. The horizontal trace across the back is *evidently at a lower level* than the wound in front, and as the trace of blood on the back is horizontal, not slanting, it could not come from the wound in front. This bears out what Teresa Neumann and Catherine Emmerich say that they saw the soldier with the lance on horseback and that the thrust of the lance was downwards.

"YOU SHALL NOT BREAK A BONE OF HIM"

St. John is here quoting the prophet Isaias. Dr. Barbet quotes this prophecy and yet he holds that the nose of Our Divine Saviour was fractured. Contrary to Dr. Barbet other surgeons hold that the heel of the hand can be nailed without breaking any bones. A look at a skeleton will not confirm the claim of Dr. Barbet. The Shroud and the Contemplatives give evidence that the heel of the hand and not the wrist was nailed.